A Visit to INDIA

NORTH AMERICA

EUROPE

ASIA

AFRICA

INDIA

SOUTH AMERICA

AUSTRALIA

Peter & Connie Roop

Heinemann
LIBRARY

First published in Great Britain by Heinemann Library
Halley Court, Jordan Hill, Oxford OX2 8EJ
a division of Reed Educational and Professional Publishing Ltd.
Heinemann is a registered trademark of Reed Educational & Professional Publishing Limited.

OXFORD MELBOURNE AUCKLAND KUALA LUMPUR
SINGAPORE IBADAN NAIROBI KAMPALA JOHANNESBURG
GABORONE PORTSMOUTH NH CHICAGO

Designed by AMR
Illustrations by Art Construction
Printed in Hong Kong / China

02 01
10 9 8 7 6 5 4 3 2

ISBN 0 431 08318 5
This title is also available in a hardback library edition (ISBN 0 431 08309 6).

British Library Cataloguing in Publication Data

Roop, Peter
 A visit to India
 1. India – Social conditions – 1974 –   – Juvenile literature
 2. India – Geography – Juvenile literature
 3. India – Social life and customs – Juvenile literature
 I.Title II.India
 954·.052

Acknowledgements
The Publishers would like to thank the following for permission to reproduce photographs:
J Allan Cash Ltd: pp7, 8, 14, 15, 18, 21, 28, 29; Hutchison Library: J Horner pp10, 23, J Highet p25,
L Taylor p22; Images of India: pp13, 27; Magnum: R Raghu pp19, 24; Panos Pictures: S Anwar p6,
R Berriedale-Johnson p5, N Durrell-McKenna p12, J Horner p16, Z Nelson p11, D O'Leary pp17, 20,
P Smith pp9, 26

Cover photograph reproduced with permission of Spectrum Colour Library

Every effort has been made to contact copyright holders of any material reproduced in this
book. Any omissions will be rectified in subsequent printings if notice is given to the Publisher.

Any words appearing in bold, **like this**, are explained in the Glossary.

Contents

India

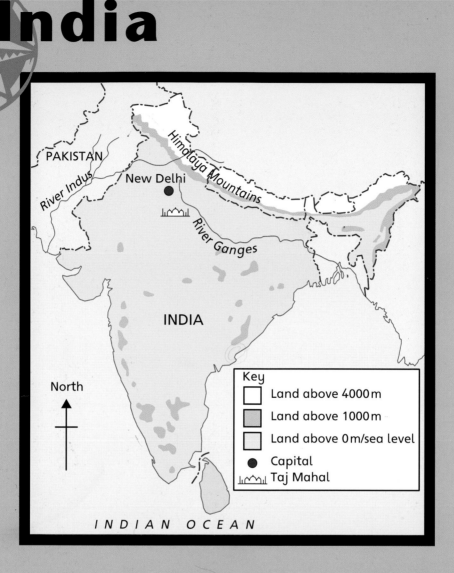

India takes its name from the River Indus.
This river runs through Pakistan, which
used to be part of India. India is in Asia.
It is shaped like a diamond.

Many people live in India. Only China has more people than India. Most Indians live in the country but the cities are very crowded.

Land

India has three main types of land.
In the north of the country are the
Himalaya Mountains. These are the
highest mountains in the world.

The middle of India forms the largest
plain in the world. The other part of
India is the **peninsula**. It has high, flat
mountains and many miles of
beautiful seashore.

Landmarks

The Taj Mahal is India's most famous building. It was built 300 years ago in memory of a much loved queen, called Mumtaz Mahal.

The River Ganges is a long, wide river. To many Indians it is a holy river and there are many places along its banks where people pray and wash in it.

Homes

In the cities people live in small flats. Many poor people live in huts or tents or have no homes at all. It is very dangerous for these people during the **monsoon season**.

Most people live in country villages.
Some homes are made of **bamboo** or
home-made clay bricks. Large families
live together in one building.

Food

Many Indians eat only vegetables and seafood, cooked with fresh spices. Rice or bread is served with every meal. Indian breads are round and flat.

A very popular dish is tandoori, which is meat cooked in a very hot, clay oven. Another favourite meal is dhal, a thick lentil soup eaten with bread.

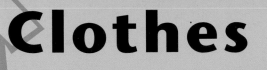

Clothes

Most Indian women wear **saris**. They are cool and comfortable. They can be very plain for work, or **embroidered** in beautiful colours for special days.

Some men wear loose trousers called pajamas. Farmers wear dhotis, which are cloths tied round their waist. In the cities many people wear clothes like yours.

15

Work

Most Indians are farmers. They grow rice, tea, sugar cane, wheat, fruit and vegetables. They can grow two **crops** a year in the hot, wet weather.

Some people work in **factories** and make
cloth, computers, bicycles, cars and tools.
Many people make and sell things from
their own home.

Transport

In the crowded streets you will see
lorries, cars, scooters, bicycles, rickshaws
(three-wheeled bicycles for passengers
or heavy loads) and people on foot.

Most trains and buses are so full that people ride on the roof. India's rivers are also very busy. Large and small boats carry people and **cargo** along them.

There are many different kinds of Indian people. Each group has its own **customs** and beliefs. Over 75 languages are spoken in India.

Hindi is the most important language in India. Hindi and English are taught in schools so that Indians can speak to each other whatever their language.

School

Children go to school from the age
of 6 to 14. They study Hindi, English,
maths, history and geography.

Many children are too poor to go to school. Their families need them to stay at home and help farm or beg in the streets.

Free time

Indians are very keen cricketers. Children practise on the streets with a bat and ball. Other popular sports are hockey, badminton, polo and football (soccer).

One of the favourite entertainments in India is going to the cinema. Indian film stars are treated like heroes. Families also enjoy funfairs in the early evening.

Celebrations

The different **religions** in India each have many festivals. Diwali is the Hindu New Year. It lasts for five days. Many lamps and fireworks make it a festival of light.

Hindus also believe that cows are holy.
The festival of Pongal honours them.
The cows are washed, painted and
decorated with flowers.

The Arts

Many Indians enjoy making beautiful
things from metal, wood, stone or
cloth. Their paintings and clothes use
bright colours and detailed patterns.

The sitar is a famous Indian instrument.
It is like a guitar with up to 26 strings.
Sometimes its music is used for dancing
to. These dances often tell old stories.

Factfile

Name   The full name of India is the Republic of India.

Capital   The **capital** of India is New Delhi.

Language   Most Indians speak Hindi and some English, but there are 75 other main types of language spoken in India.

Population There are about 950 million people living in India.

Money   Instead of the dollar or pound, the Indians have the rupee.

Religion   Most Indians believe in Hinduism (which worships many gods). As well as Hindus there are also some Muslims, Christians and Sikhs.

Products   India produces lots of rice, wheat, tea, sugar, coffee, jewellery, clothes and machinery.

Words you can learn

ek (ik)   one
do (daw)   two
tin (dean)   three
namaste (nahm-as-teh)   hello
namaste   goodbye
shukrinya   thank you
mehabani seh (meha-bani-seh)   please

Glossary

bamboo	a tall plant with a long, strong stem
capital	the city where the government is based
cargo	things that are transported
crops	the plants that are grown and harvested
customs	the way people do things
embroidered	stitches used to decorate material
factories	places where many of the same things are made
lentil	a kind of bean
monsoon season	a time of very rainy weather
peninsula	land with water on three sides
plain	an area of open, flat land
religions	what people believe in
saris	long pieces of cloth wrapped around the waist and shoulders

Index